ANIMALS ATTACK!

Alligators

Lorie Garver

**KIDHAVEN
PRESS™**

THOMSON
™
GALE

San Diego • Detroit • New York • San Francisco • Cleveland
New Haven, Conn. • Waterville, Maine • London • Munich

*Special thanks to Skulls Unlimited International
for their continued generosity.*

For more information, contact
KidHaven Press
27500 Drake Rd.
Farmington Hills, MI 48331-3535
Or you can visit our Internet site at http://www.gale.com

LIBRARY OF CONGRESS CATALOGING-IN-PUBLICATION DATA

Garver, Lorie.
  Alligators / by Lorie Garver.
    p. cm.—(Animals attack)
  Summary: Describes the habits and behavior of animals, emphasizing how
dangerous they can be, and relates true stories of alligator attacks.
  Includes bibliographical references and index.
    ISBN 0-7377-1524-3 (hardback : alk. paper)
    1. Alligator attacks—United States—Juvenile literature. 2. Alligators—United
States—Juvenile literature. [1. Alligators. 2. Alligator attacks.] I. Title. II. Series.
  QL666.C925G38 2004
  597.98'4—dc22
                                                                      2003012903

Printed in the United States of America

Contents

Chapter 1
A Hardy, Hungry Beast   4

Chapter 2
Please Do Not Feed the Alligators   13

Chapter 3
POSTED: No Swimming or Wading
from Dusk to Dawn   22

Chapter 4
Never Let Down Your Guard   30

Glossary   41
For Further Exploration   43
Index   45
Picture Credits   47
About the Author   48

Chapter 1

A Hardy, Hungry Beast

An alligator is born ready to attack. As soon as it hatches from an egg, it snaps and snarls and will bite a handler with its needle-sharp baby teeth. As it grows, an alligator's appearance, size, speed, strength, and senses allow it to attack and eat whatever it chooses.

Alligators are members of the Crocodylia order of **reptiles**. Of the alligator **species** only the American is a threat to humans.

Most American alligators are found in the southeastern United States from Texas to Virginia. Florida has more alligators than any other state. Experts estimate that over 1 million alligators live in the swampy

Everglades National Park on the southern tip of Florida.

A million alligators need a great deal of food, and no person or animal is safe from becoming an alligator's meal. These creatures are not picky eaters. They feed on almost anything they have a chance to capture and eat: birds, fish, snakes, turtles, and small mammals.

A hungry alligator lunges for a fish. Alligators will eat anything they can catch.

Alligators also attack to protect their **territory**. They threaten anything seen as an invader to their **habitat**. They have even attacked cars and boats, crunching and puncturing bumpers and outboard motors with the strength of their bite.

A Modern Day Prehistoric Beast

Alligators look like **ancient** creatures from the days of dinosaurs. This is because their **ancestors** date back to **prehistoric** times. Unlike dinosaurs, alligators successfully adapted to changes in climate, ge-

A prehistoric alligator, Phobosuchus, snarls at an intruding Chasmosaurus.

ography, and habitat, allowing these hardy beasts to survive for the past 200 million years. It is amazing that the alligator has been able to survive for millions of years. But the alligator is built to survive.

The alligator's mighty jaws may be its most remarkable feature: a wide, flat, U-shaped **snout** and broad head filled with eighty dull, cone-shaped teeth. Although the teeth are not sharp, the power of the jaw makes the teeth a deadly weapon. Alligator jaws have up to three thousand pounds of pressure per square inch of closing power. That is four times the pressure of a large dog's bite! The alligator's bite is so strong that the beast can grab an animal the size

Alligators have heavy heads and thick necks, and grow from twelve to fourteen feet in length.

of a horse and snap its neck in a single crushing chomp.

Another key to the alligator's survival is size. Wild alligators in the United States can grow to over twelve feet in length and weigh as much as 600 pounds. The longest Florida alligator found so far was more than fourteen feet long when it was captured, and the most massive was one that weighed 1,040 pounds—nearly half a ton.

The alligator has a heavy head, thick neck, and four short, powerful legs. A strong, muscular tail makes up half of its length. As an amphibian the alligator can live both on land and in water.

Thick scales in different shapes and strengths cover the alligator's body. These tough, armorlike scales, called **scutes**, help the alligator to survive. Scutes keep the alligator's hide from drying out and also protect it from its enemies.

Spring and Summer: Seasons for Attacks

An alligator's behavior changes as the seasons of the year change. Like other reptiles the outside temperature affects their body temperature. During cold weather an alligator's body temperature drops. While alligators do not hibernate, they do become sluggish and slow during cold weather. They rarely eat from October to April. But when it gets warm outside, their body temperature rises, signaling them to become active and search for food.

The warm weather also signals an alligator's mating season. Alligators become brutally aggressive as they search for mates, and show off by **bellowing** and slapping their heads on the surface of the water. They are also more likely to attack during this period.

After mating, a female becomes fiercely protective of her eggs and her **hatchling** babies. Up to seventy eggs are laid in a nest she builds on the water's edge. She guards them closely and threatens any human or animal that comes near by hissing, puffing up her body, and snapping her jaws.

Alligators are aggressive during mating season in order to protect their species, but they are even more aggressive when they are hungry and stalk their **prey**.

A hatchling alligator rests at the water's edge, not far from its protective mother (background).

A sneaky alligator floats motionless in the water. Alligators are well camouflaged.

Born to Be Silent, Sneaky, and Swift

An alligator has several advantages leading up to an attack. It lurks in water, unmoving, for hours at a time. Since its eyes, ears, and nostrils are located on top of its head, the alligator can leave only the top of its head peeking above water. It listens, watches, and waits, using its keen senses to detect its next meal.

The alligator is well **camouflaged** since its skin is usually the same color as the water it swims in. The alligator's head looks like a harmless, bumpy log floating in the water.

Speed and strength are two more advantages the alligator has as an attacker. If near the water's edge,

A captive alligator shoots straight out of the water during feeding time.

an alligator uses its strong, muscular tail and lightning speed to propel itself out of the water and up the beach. It seems to shoot straight out of the water to snatch a victim.

Considering an alligator's physical features, fiercely protective mating and nesting behaviors, and vicious attack abilities, it is easy to see how this prehistoric creature continues to survive and thrive in modern times.

Chapter 2

Please Do Not Feed the Alligators

Feeding alligators is a dangerous practice. Alligators can become dependent on human food, lose their fear of humans, and therefore become more aggressive and dangerous. In several states it is illegal to feed alligators. When a person breaks this law in Florida and is caught, the fine is five hundred dollars with a sixty-day jail sentence.

Even so, many people ignore these laws and feed alligators along riverbanks, lakeshores, and **bayous**. Children and adults throw hamburgers, hot dogs, fish, chicken, marshmallows, sandwiches, and pet food to alligators. Dumping fish bait and fish heads

A tourist feeds a twelve-foot alligator. Feeding wild alligators is illegal in many states where the reptiles are common.

in lakes and rivers also provides easy food and attracts alligators to areas where humans gather.

Sometimes a home owner feeds an alligator when it wanders into the yard. After this the reptile sees people and thinks of food. It **salivates**, snaps, and swallows when it sees a person. It may approach a child or adult aggressively, expecting a handout, then turn mean and vicious. Alligators that are used to eating human food have been known to react to the crumpling sound of a potato chip bag.

Sadly, alligators that lose their fear of humans must be destroyed by wildlife officials. They are too dangerous. Many attacks can be traced to an alligator having been fed by humans.

An Innocent Victim

Joe Elam was feeding bread crumbs to pet birds and fish in his yard at Hilton Head, South Carolina, when he was attacked by an eight-foot alligator. The creature crept into his yard from a nearby **lagoon** on a warm Saturday evening in June and charged the man.

Elam tried to escape by running away. When he tripped the alligator bit him on his right leg. Elam used his fists to pound on the creature's eyes and nose until it let go and crept back to the water.

Elam had a six-inch cut on his calf, bite marks on his shin and behind his knee, and bruised muscles. He also broke his left collarbone and one of his toes when he fell.

A wildlife agent had to shoot and kill the alligator because it had lost its fear of humans. A neighbor reported that the alligator had been in the area for at least ten years, becoming bolder and bolder as people sometimes fed it.

Human Tug-of-War

Dagmar Dow and her family moved from Arizona to Lake Como, north of Tampa, Florida. Dow, her husband, and three sons lived in Florida for only six months when disaster struck. One hot June afternoon

Dagmar and her husband floated in chest-deep water in the thirty-five acre lake, practicing for an upcoming **scuba diving** lesson in the Florida Keys. Their youngest son watched from a fenced-in section near the lake's shore.

Dagmar never saw the nearly ten-foot alligator that pulled her underwater and almost bit off her foot. Her husband, Ray, described the attack like a scene from the movie *Jaws* when his wife went straight down into the water as if sucked under by a giant vacuum cleaner.

He dove to where she disappeared, grabbed her, and began kicking whatever was clutching her. He did not think of an alligator; he only knew something had grabbed her from beneath and was holding her. He pulled one way and the creature released her foot. The alligator struck again, grabbing onto one of Dagmar's arms. Ray continued to pull on his wife and kick the creature in its face. It let go of the woman when the muscle tore loose from her arm. The entire attack lasted less than forty-five seconds.

Ray grabbed his bleeding wife around her waist and pulled her to shore. That was when they saw and realized that she was badly hurt. Dagmar's foot was hanging on by a couple of pieces of flesh and **sinew**. Her arm was bleeding from the shoulder to the elbow.

Dagmar was in **shock**. At first she did not feel much pain. Her husband called the **paramedics** and soon she was airlifted to a nearby hospital and rushed into surgery.

Meanwhile, the alligator could be seen on the surface of the water for the first time. It floated about forty feet from the lake's edge and appeared to be attracted by the blood in the water. The creature circled closer to shore then paced on the beach until a hunter destroyed the 350-pound animal a few hours later.

The Dows learned from Florida wildlife officials that people who lived on the lake had been feeding the alligator that attacked Dagmar. Residents reported that several small alligators lived in the lake, but they had never been a problem. The Dows were aware of these smaller alligators, but had never seen the ten-foot creature that attacked Dagmar.

A group of alligators rests on a sandy beach. Feeding alligators can cause the animals to lose their fear of humans.

Six months after the attack, Dagmar Dow was home in the Lake Como community, recovering from a sixth and final surgery. Her right forearm had a long gash, and a chunk of flesh was gone from her **triceps** muscle. Her left ankle was missing some bone fragments, but doctors had saved her foot. Scars criss-crossed her skin like a spider's web. But, she is lucky to be alive.

In the tug-of-war contest between a monster-size, aggressive reptile and Ray, her 180-pound, six-foot-tall husband, Dagmar Dow was the winner.

An Uncle's Superhuman Strength

Kindergartner Jesse Valdez liked to play with his older brother, Jose, near a canal just a few yards away from his family's front door in Clewiston, Florida. The neighborhood children enjoyed gathering at this front-yard playground until one Saturday afternoon in May when a ten-foot, 325-pound alligator snatched Jesse from the water's edge.

Shortly before the alligator attacked the young boy, witnesses saw people throwing live chickens at the creature. It appeared comfortable to be so close to people. When Jesse tripped on a tree root and tumbled down the canal bank, the alligator was right there to lunge and grab him in its steel-trap-like jaws.

Jose was a few doors away and heard his brother scream. He ran to the spot on the canal bank and saw the little boy in the mouth of the alligator.

Built to Attack!

Flat, U-shaped snout and eighty cone-shaped teeth for grabbing prey.

Thick scales act as armor.

Eyes, ears, and nose located on top of the head allow the alligator to see, hear, and breathe while underwater.

Strong legs and powerful tail help the alligator catch prey with great speed.

Huge jaws chomp prey with thousands of pounds of pressure per square inch.

Jesse's uncle, Ever Vasquez, heard the child scream, too. He leaped into the waist-deep water of the canal to rescue his little nephew. Vasquez was only 140 pounds and five feet, five inches tall–less than half the size of the alligator. He grabbed Jesse's hand while the alligator held onto the boy's leg. Vasquez snatched rocks and sticks, anything he could find, and hit the animal on the head. He managed to loosen Jesse from the alligator's grip.

But the alligator did not give up. It struck again, jerking Jesse away from his uncle's hold, this time chomping down on the boy's shoulder. Vasquez went after the alligator again, pulled Jesse away from the creature, and scrambled out of the canal with his nephew in his arms.

A man feeds an alligator at an alligator farm. Feeding alligators can be extremely dangerous.

Jesse and his uncle were taken to a local hospital for treatment of their wounds. Jesse had puncture wounds to his right shoulder, right thigh, and back. His uncle had a bite wound on his hand. Both were treated and allowed to go home.

When wildlife officials arrived to capture the alligator, they knew it was being fed by humans because it took their bait so easily. The officials also noticed how fat the creature's tail was, another sign of being fed by people.

Two days after the attack, Jesse was still swollen, bruised, and sore from throbbing cuts. He did not remember much about the attack, and did not want to talk about it. He did know, however, that he wanted nothing to do with alligators.

Doctors told Jesse's mother it was a miracle that her son survived the attack. She and the entire neighborhood considered Ever Vasquez a hero.

Until the awful attack Vasquez had never seen an alligator. He was surprised by the creature's size once he got a good look at it. He remembered only that he acted **instinctively**, fighting with all of his might to save his little nephew. Officials said that Vasquez did exactly the right thing–fighting back to confuse the alligator, making it think it attacked something too big to handle.

Joe Elam, Dagmar Dow, and Jesse Valdez suffered the terrifying results of other people who foolishly, dangerously, and illegally fed alligators.

Chapter 3

POSTED: No Swimming or Wading from Dusk to Dawn

Nothing feels as good at the end of a hot, sticky summer day as an evening swim in a cool river or lake. In Florida, however, this enjoyable experience is dangerous, since a swimmer could share an evening dip with alligators. The reptiles are found in nearly every body of water in the state and are most active at night. Many alligator attacks occur when people choose to swim, wade, or even walk along the water's edge in the evening.

Even with posted signs and active public service warnings, people still choose to swim in the evenings. Some have terrifying experiences.

A Strong Young Man

If Daniel Denslinger had not been such a large, strong fourteen year old, he probably would not have survived an alligator attack one summer night in Punta Gorda, Florida. The battle between reptile and teenager might have had a different ending.

Daniel and two friends were swimming and splashing in Preacher's Lake when a nine-and-a-half-foot, 300-pound creature pulled Daniel under the

Alligator eyes glow at dusk in a Florida swamp. Alligators are most active at night.

water by biting him in both legs. The teenager, a strapping six feet and 220 pounds, wrestled the alligator's jaws open and swam away. He had fourteen stitches and was allowed to go home from a local hospital.

A Sneaky Beach Attack

Tammy Woehle thought it would be safe to walk her dog, Lady, just before nightfall on Big Talbot Island's

A nighttime encounter with an alligator is a terrifying experience.

sandy beach near Jacksonville, Florida. After all, it was still light out, and she was away from high grasses and the water's edge.

She did not see or hear an eight-foot-long creature creeping up to her. The alligator chomped down on her left thigh, and Tammy fell to the ground. The alligator unexpectedly released her leg, giving her an opportunity to scoot away from the creature and run to safety.

She was treated for a six-inch-long wound at a local hospital and allowed to go home. Doctors and nurses told her the alligator ripped away a portion of her leg muscle. They also told her she was very lucky. Tammy certainly agreed.

His Head Was in the Alligator's Jaws

Frank Dotson's neighbors in the small town of Dunnellon, Florida, warned him about swimming in the Withlacoochee River. The yellow-brown water of the river was known to be full of alligators.

For fifteen years, though, Dotson swam every evening in the Withlacoochee with his two mixed-breed dogs, Nikki and Billy-Jack. He shrugged off his neighbors' concerns and continued to enjoy his nightly swims.

One August night a huge alligator came out of nowhere and chomped down on Frank's head. The man managed to free himself and swim to shore. He climbed from the water and began stumbling home through a wooded area.

A neighbor heard Frank's weak cries for help and led him to the front porch. He wrapped a towel around the man's bleeding head. When emergency medical technicians arrived, Frank was airlifted to a local hospital. The right side of his face was severely damaged and his ear was split.

That night trappers from the Florida Fish and Wildlife **Conservation** Commission caught and killed three alligators. They ranged in size from seven and a half to eleven feet. There was no evidence to link any of the three to the attack on Frank Dotson, but officials felt that one of them was the likely culprit.

Although no warning signs were posted about alligators, the chilling close call was a lesson for all residents in the area.

A Best Friend Becomes a Hero

It was a typical hot August night at Little Lake Conway near Orlando, Florida. Fourteen-year-old Edna Wilks and five of her friends were splashing and playing on boogie boards in five feet of water about thirty feet from the lakeshore.

Edna felt a strong pull on the arm she was dangling in the water. At first she thought it was one of her friends and told him to stop. She turned to look at him, saw the snout of an alligator, and realized it was not her friend. The creature jerked her underwater and began the rapid **death spin**, a technique alligators use to drown their prey.

Alligators are fierce hunters, especially underwater.

Edna was sure she was going to die. The alligator spun her around and around underwater. She heard a loud crack as the bones in her arm snapped in the alligator's powerful jaws. She surfaced with her arm still in the alligator's mouth. After taking a deep breath, Edna used her free hand to pry the creature's mouth open. The animal finally released her arm.

During the attack the other children raced to shore. All but one, Amanda Valance, Edna's best friend. Amanda was a few feet away and watched

An alligator's powerful jaws can easily crush human bones.

frozen in horror as her friend was attacked. After Edna worked herself free, Amanda grabbed her and propped her up on one of the boards. She began pushing and pulling Edna toward shore.

At first Edna tried to lift her injured arm. She panicked when she could not see her arm below the elbow. She thought it was gone, bitten off by the alligator. As she kicked and paddled toward shore on a boogie board, she realized her fingers were wiggling. She knew then that her lower arm was still attached. She used her good arm to hold the bleeding arm and leaned on the board to swim to shore.

Amanda watched the alligator turn and follow them. It disappeared. She was terrified it would attack again, but stayed by her friend's side to take her to shore. Amanda continued to help Edna by encouraging her. She did not want to see her friend die.

The other children ran across the lake road to Edna's house, screaming for her mother. When Mrs. Wilks ran to the water's edge, she saw a large alligator floating among the empty boogie boards.

Edna was taken to a local hospital. She had lost so much blood that she had no blood pressure when she arrived. She was given blood **transfusions** and treated for deep cuts and broken bones in her left forearm. Doctors took her into surgery several times to give the wound a deep cleaning due to bacteria in the lake and in the alligator's mouth.

Edna knew she was a very lucky girl. She also felt lucky to have a brave, devoted friend who stayed by her side during this most frightening experience.

Chapter 4

Never Let Down Your Guard

People who live in the southeastern United States work and play near alligators every day. The two species–alligators and humans–have learned to **co-exist**. Sometimes, however, this peaceful coexistence leads to a false sense of security. People become too brave when they are around alligators so often and nothing dangerous happens.

But people should never let down their guard around these creatures and cannot become careless in their habits. Alligators are wild, meat-eating animals that act instinctively, leading to attacks for no reason but to eat. In the stories of many attacks, the person who was attacked or someone who saw the attack realized afterward that something might have prevented the tragic incident.

When entering the world of the alligator, it pays to be cautious and respectful.

Routine Maintenance Work

Don Goodman was always careful to search for stray alligators before stepping into the water-lily pond at the Kanapaha **Botanical Gardens** in Gainesville, Florida. After all, for nearly twenty-five years, he had been director of the sixty-two-acre park where a few alligators frequently traveled from a nearby lake to

A ferocious alligator snaps at the camera. Alligators are wild, unpredictable creatures.

slink around in the park's ponds. One hot September afternoon, though, Don did not look closely enough.

For several months a large alligator had been living in the water garden. Nicknamed Mojo by park employees, the creature's size of eleven feet and four hundred pounds was frightening, but the alligator was not viewed as threatening. It had not made any moves toward anyone or anything–until that particular Monday afternoon in September.

A juvenile alligator struggles to free itself after being captured.

Don entered waist-deep water to remove **algae** from the park's prize water lilies. As he walked through the pond, he felt a most unusual sensation—he thought his right arm was being twisted off. Due to shock he felt no pain, but he sensed the twisting and saw a great deal of blood.

Don made a split-second decision. He knew he had to do something to rescue himself, and that choice was to give up all of him or part of him to the creature. Don chose to pull free, leaving his arm in the alligator's jaws, but giving him a chance to escape.

He yelled for help. His fellow employees came, tied a **tourniquet** on his wound below the elbow, and rushed him to the hospital. Officials from the Florida Fish and Wildlife Conservation Commission raced to the park to trap the alligator and try to get Don's severed arm back.

Trappers were sent to the scene. They launched a boat into the shallow pond and **harpooned** the alligator. The frenzied creature rammed the boat, knocking a trapper into the water. The trapper's partner pulled him back into the boat while the alligator tried to chomp him.

When the trappers dragged the alligator out of the pond, they shot it and slit open its stomach. An official reached in, found Don's arm, placed it carefully in a bag, and took it to the hospital. Surgeons examined it and saw how badly the tissue was shredded and the muscles were torn. They were also concerned about infection from bacteria in the alligator's

Range of the American Alligator

MISSOURI

KENTUCKY

VIRGINIA

OKLAHOMA

ARKANSAS

TENNESSEE

NORTH CAROLINA

SOUTH CAROLINA

ALABAMA

GEORGIA

MISSISSIPPI

Atlantic Ocean

TEXAS

LOUISIANA

Gulf of Mexico

FLORIDA

stomach. They decided the arm was too damaged to reattach.

Don was fitted with an artificial arm, and he returned to his job. Another large alligator in the park was destroyed, just to be safe, and the third one was taken to Gatorland, a theme park in Orlando, Florida.

Don Goodman considered himself lucky. He lost only an arm, not his life, to an alligator.

An Out-of-Character Attack

On a sunny February day in Englewood, Florida, Helen Couto decided to trim the palmetto bushes near her home. She did not have alligators on her mind. It was the middle of the day, it was too early in the spring for reptiles to be active, and she was working in her own yard. She felt safe.

While she worked a small alligator latched on to her arm just below the elbow and tried to drag her to a nearby pond. When neighbors heard her chilling screams, they came to her rescue. One grabbed Helen's ankles and pulled her and the creature away from the water. Another picked up a branch that Helen had been cutting and threw it on the alligator's eyes. The creature clamped down, tore off the lower part of Helen's arm, and swam away.

While Helen was taken to the hospital, a deputy shot and killed the alligator. Wildlife officials cut the creature open to get the arm. But, like Don Goodman, Helen Couto's arm was too damaged for doctors to reattach.

Wildlife officials retrieve Helen Couto's arm from the stomach of the alligator that attacked her.

Helen learned that, even in the safety of her own backyard, she can never let down her guard.

Just a Typical Family Outing on Father's Day

Ten-year-old Megan Roe was happy to spend time with her father and brother on Father's Day at Hog Island in the Withlacoochee River, a popular park where families gathered for swimming and picnicking. No one would have guessed that a pleasant Sunday afternoon would turn into a terrifying experience for Megan, her father, and her brother.

Eric, Megan's brother, floated on a rubber raft in the river. Megan swam next to him in three feet of water. Mr. Roe was in front of his children, swimming a few feet away. They noticed a giant log floating near them.

But it was not a log. It was an eleven-foot, four-hundred-pound alligator. It lunged and clamped its deadly jaws around Megan's leg. It started to drag her into deeper water.

Mr. Roe turned, grabbed his daughter, and began to wrestle her away from the reptile. Eric rolled off his raft and fought the alligator, too. Megan's father pulled her toward shore, but the alligator would not let go. Desperate to save his daughter, Megan's quick-thinking father made a lucky guess. He poked the beast in the eye with his bare fingers. When its eye was gouged, the alligator released its viselike

David Peters was attacked while rescuing his dog from an aggressive alligator.

hold on the girl. Mr. Roe pulled his daughter out of the water and onto the riverbank.

Megan was cut and bleeding. Her father wrapped her in a towel and drove her to an area hospital. Emergency room doctors and nurses stopped the bleeding. Shortly after that Megan was taken to another hospital where she stayed for several days. She had surgery to clean the wound. Doctors used twenty-four stitches to repair the tears in her skin and muscle.

Officials closed the park on Hog Island while they searched the river for the alligator. They found it about twenty yards from the scene of the attack and killed it. Although no physical evidence linked the creature to Megan's attack, it was the only large alligator in the area. Officials were certain it was the attacker.

A Florida man holds tightly to a captured alligator's tail. The number of alligator attacks in Florida increases every year.

One of the Florida Fish and Wildlife Conservation Commissioners felt that the alligator saw Megan as another alligator invading its territory. Megan's father and brother saved her life by fighting the creature and making as much noise and confusion as possible.

Megan Roe recovered from her frightening encounter with an alligator. Nearly a year after the attack, she no longer swam in rivers or lakes, preferring clear springs at a local park. Based on her experience, she warned people against swimming in murky water that might keep them from seeing what may be hiding below the surface.

Why So Many Attacks?

Alligator attacks that seem to happen for no reason are increasing in Florida. For more than fifty years Florida agencies have kept careful records of these incidents. For a long time about five people were attacked each year. In the last few years, however, that number has suddenly jumped to twelve, seventeen, and even twenty-three attacks each year.

Not all alligator attacks end with victims making a full recovery, escaping with scars, or losing only an arm. Since 1948 twelve people have been killed in Florida by alligators. The state's residents and tourists are worried by frequent reports of vicious alligator aggression.

Experts believe that attacks have increased as people and alligators compete for space. Florida is a

A wild alligator crosses a road. Alligator attacks will continue to increase as people and alligators compete for space.

popular place for retirement and outdoor fun. When people move to the state, many want homes near water, often built in areas that were once homes to alligators. As swamplands become suburbs, alligators are relocated to unfamiliar territory. They wander instinctively, trying to find their original homes, and sometimes find themselves on golf courses or airport runways, near shopping malls, and even in neighborhood pools and ponds.

As more people live and play where alligators roam, more attacks will happen.

Glossary

algae: A seaweedlike growth found in ponds and other bodies of water.

ancestor: A long-ago relative of an existing person or animal.

ancient: Lived for many years or in a time early in history.

bayou: A creek or marshy body of water that usually feeds into a river.

bellow: A loud, deep, hollow sound.

botanical garden: A garden or park for the study and display of special plants.

camouflage: Physical characteristics that allow an animal to blend into its surroundings for protection.

coexist: To live in the same area.

conservation: The careful protection of animals and plants.

death spin: A spinning move used by an alligator to drown a victim.

habitat: An area where an animal naturally lives and grows.

harpoon: A spear used to hunt large water creatures.

hatchling: A baby alligator.

instinct: Behavior that occurs quickly and naturally without thinking.

lagoon: A shallow pond, artificial or natural, often connected to a larger body of water.

paramedic: A specially trained medical assistant licensed to give emergency treatment.

prehistoric: Time periods before written history.

prey: An animal that is hunted, killed, and eaten by another animal.

reptile: A cold-blooded animal such as an alligator, crocodile, turtle, snake, or lizard.

salivate: To drool when food is present.

scuba diving: Swimming with a device that delivers oxygen for breathing underwater.

scute: A large, bony scale.

shock: The body's reaction to severe injury or burns, which may cause the victim to have memory loss, no feeling of pain, and great confusion.

sinew: A strong band of tissue that connects muscle with bone.

snout: The nose of an animal.

species: A group of creatures with common characteristics and a common name.

territory: An area where an animal lives and that is defended by that animal.

tourniquet: A tightly twisted bandage used to stop bleeding.

transfusion: The process of putting blood into the body of a person or animal through a vein.

triceps: A large muscle along the back of the upper arm.

For Further Exploration

Books

Missy Allen and Michel Peissel. *Encyclopedia of Danger: Dangerous Reptilian Creatures.* New York: Chelsea House, 1993. This book uses vivid language and stories, along with maps, illustrations, and colorful symbols, to share the dangers of twenty-five of the most threatening reptiles.

Patrick J. Fitzgerald, *Croc and Gator Attacks.* New York: Childrens, 2000. This book discusses the history of and reasons for crocodile and alligator attacks on humans. It has stories of attacks, photographs, sidebars, a fact sheet, and a glossary.

Video Sources

Alligator and Crocodile Adventures (videocassette), National Audubon Society, 1997. In a series designed for family viewing, this title has lively narration and colorful images that describe the similarities and differences between alligators and crocodiles.

Realm of the Alligator (videocassette), National Geographic Society, 1986. Scientists study the behavior of alligators by entering the mysterious wilderness of Okefenokee, seven hundred miles of swampland on the Georgia-Florida state border.

Websites

Animal Planet, "Ferocious Crocs: Ask a Croc Expert." (www.animal.discovery.com).

Crocodilians: Natural History and Conservation (www.crocodilian.com). Created by Dr. Adam Britton, research officer for Wildlife Management International, this website is a rich collection of information about crocodilians–their species, biology, conservation, how they communicate, and captive care.

DISASTER! Magazine, "Surviving a Gator Attack." (www.disastermagazine.com).

Fish and Wildlife Conservation Commission, "Living with Alligators." (www.wld.fwc.state.fl.us).

The Gator Hole (http://home.cfl.rr.com). A website devoted to everything about alligators–relatives, habitats, habits, myths and facts, and more. A collection of clickable photographs is included.

Pinellas County Extension Home Page, "Keeping out of the Alligator's Food Web." (http://coop.co.pinellas.fl.us).

Tripod Home Page, "The Alligator." (www.members.tripod.com).

Index

American alligators, 4
ancestors, 6–7
attacks
  death spins, 26–27, 39
  humans feeding
    alligators and, 15, 17,
    21
  on humans near water,
    18, 20, 24–25
  on humans swimming,
    16, 22–24, 25–28,
    36–37
  on humans working,
    31–35
  increase in, 39–40
  during mating season,
    9–10
  stalking, 11–12

behavior, seasons and,
  9–10
bite, 7–8
body, 7–9, 12

camouflage, 11
Couto, Helen, 34–35

death spins, 26–27, 39
Denslinger, Daniel,
  23–24
Dotson, Frank, 25–26
Dow, Dagmar, 15–18
Dow, Ray, 16–18

Everglades National
  Park, Florida, 4–5

Florida
  Everglades National
    Park, 4–5
  feeding alligators in,
    13–15, 17, 21
  Fish and Wildlife
    Conservation
    Commission, 26, 33
  Kanapaha Botanical
    Gardens, 31

Goodman, Don, 31–34

habitat, 4–5, 6, 40
hatchlings, 4, 10
humans
  fear of, 15
  feeding alligators,
    13–15, 17, 21
  see also attacks, on
  humans

jaws, 7–8

Kanapaha Botanical
  Gardens, Florida, 31

legs, 9

mating, 9
Mojo (alligator), 32

prey, 5

range, 4–5
reptiles, 4
Roe, Eric, 36, 39

Roe, Megan, 36–37, 39
Roe, Mr. (Megan's
  father), 36–37, 39

scutes, 9
size, 8–9
snout, 7
speed, 11
stalking, 11–12
strength, 7–8, 11–12
swimming, 16, 22–24,
  25–28, 36–37

tail, 9, 12
teeth, 7
territory, 6

Valance, Amanda,
  27–28
Valdez, Jesse, 18, 20–21
Valdez, Jose, 18
Vasquez, Ever, 20–21

Wilks, Edna, 26–29
Woehle, Tammy,
  24–25

Picture Credits

About the Author

Lorie Garver taught kindergartners through graduate students and was an elementary school principal in Indiana and Arizona. She holds degrees from DePauw University and Indiana University, and licenses from Purdue University in gifted education and school administration. She works as an education consultant and conference planner for Learning 24/7. She lives in Phoenix, Arizona, with her husband, Jim, who collaborates with her on writing, singing, and storytelling projects and workshops. Lorie writes articles for children and adult publications in her spare time. This is her first title for KidHaven Press.